And Wrap Your Arms Around Living

A COLLECTION OF POETRY

Mark Graham

Castle Knight Press
Denver, CO

Copyright © 2021 by Mark Graham.

All rights reserved. No part of this book may be reproduced in any written, electronic, recording, or photocopying without written permission of the publisher or author. The exception would be in the case of brief quotations embodied in articles or reviews and pages where permission is specifically granted by the publisher or author.

And Wrap Your Arms Around Living / Castle Knight Press
Printed in the United States of America
Front cover: Original art by Mark Graham
www.markgraham-art.com
Book Design: Graham Publishing Group

Although every precaution has been taken to verify the accuracy of the information contained herein, the author and publisher assume no responsibility for any errors or omissions. No liability is assumed for damages that may result from the use of information contained within.

And Wrap Your Arms Around Living / Mark Graham -- 1st ed.

LCCN: 2021917365
ISBN 978-1-7377229-0-8 Print Edition
ISBN 978-1-7377229-7-7 Ebook Edition

CONTENTS

And Wrap Your Arms Around Living 1
Always 2
Heart 3
What Love Is 4
Yours Alone 6
Gratitude Is Not A Shadow 7
I Am Liege 8
Yours, Mine, Ours 9
Deference 10
Perfectly Flawed 12
At Our Best 14
Hail The Curious 15
The Heartbeat Of Acceptance 16
A Thousand Joyful Moments 18
Love, Treasure, Divinity 19
No One Knows But You 20
A Blade 21
The Signpost Ahead 22
All Life Blinking Before Us 23
I Would Follow Her Anywhere 24
No Place 25
Easy 26
Humility 27
Veracity 28
Stream 29
Rising Above 30

Trinity Of Love 31
This Forever 32
Kindness Is 33
The Tool Kit Of Our Histories 34
A Storm Relentlessly Beautiful 36
Grace Is But A Shadow 37
Light Crashing From Heaven 38
Hope Is Not What Hope Is 39
What Makes Ends Meet 40
Missing Pieces 41
The Ruined Side 42
A Chance Meeting 44
Then 45
Beckon Call 46
Faith Is The Map We Never Lose 47
A Road Of A Thousand Pitfalls 48
Some Things Come Slow 49
A Thousand Transformations 50
The Day After I Saw Your Face 52
The Alchemy Of Deception 54
A Haven Known As Free Will 55
All Eyes 56
I'll Long No Longer 58
A Day As Beautiful As You 59
Goodness Is What The Man On The Corner Is Selling 60
Where The Work Lies 62
Speaking Like Song 63
Five, Four, Three, Two, One 64

Voice Reaching Heaven	65
Beyond Intimacy And Jade	66
An Ever-Evolving Canvas	68
This Long Searched For Sign	69
Buckle Up For The Ride	70
The One Thing	71
Too Often	72
Insight Tailored Just So	73
This Is Joy	74
Nothing Is Held Captive	75
My Lifeline, My Spirit	76
The Ancient World	77
To Cast Our Lot, Fearlessly	78
He Who Breathes Change	79
Blink Three Tears	80
I Yearn For Normal	82
The Silk Of Forgiveness	83
Storm The Gates	84
Alive With Lyrics	85
Diamonds Bright Within You	86
No Need To Be	88
I See It	89
For Every Change	90
Peace As Calm As Memory	92
Now There Is Time	94
Diaphanous Bleeds The Landscape	96
Nothing Changes Except The Light	97
Deep Wishes	98

Love Has No Guardian But You	99
I Tread Water	100
Sojourn To A New Life	101
Honesty Is	102
Faith Can Hold You	103
Gathering Clouds	104
Plunge, Meld, Settle	105
Splendor	106
Look	108
Hope Is A Magnet	110
I Don't Dance Anymore	111
Images Of Perfection	112
Made Whole Again	113
Its Name Is Freedom	114
Search, Or Perish	116
The Battlefield Of Completeness	117
The Purest Water	118
The Trusted Vision Of Heart	119
Never A Vendetta	120
To Spearhead A Resurrection	121
We Are One, Yet Two	122
What Cost?	123
What He Thought She Thought	124
The Bird And The Child	126
A Fighting Chance	128
Braving The Pathless	129
Now We're Onto Something	130

ALSO BY MARK GRAHAM

The Harbinger
The Missing Sixth
The Fire Theft
The Natanz Directive
The Five Portals
Parents are Diamonds, Children are Pearls

For Nobuko

The inspiration for the poems in this book – really any art form – comes from many sources. People, places, things. But most of all, family and friends. To all who have served as inspiration and motivation, my sincere thanks. -MG

AND WRAP YOUR ARMS AROUND LIVING

Listen, a trilling in the hollow,
   age beyond age,
   this place so deep inside,
   this taste of time too fleeting,
   this aching would of legacy lost.

Curious, a place carved not of hope,
   moon over sun,
   a place steeped not in expectation,
   a place seared in time made precious,
   a place verging on perfection.

And there is this:
   Time is the master of us all.
   Expectations are fraught with danger.
   Hope is a step away from imperfection.

Yet we hope, we expect, we cherish.
We move from the womb,
   fighter, emissary, survivor,
   and wrap our arms around living.

ALWAYS

What is the one word
   you wish you had said?
The one phrase
   you wish you had penned?
The one song
   you wish you had sung?

We move through our lives
   with eyes closed,
   hearts shuttered,
   souls walled from a light
   so conspicuous to one willing to see.

Me?
I wish I had said,
   "I will always celebrate your words."
I wish I had written,
   "I will always treasure your thoughts."
I wish I had sung,
   "I will always rejoice in you being you."

HEART

The Heart knows no pretense,
   Is never a party to fraud,
   Does not blur the lines
     between pure and festive.
   Does not guess,
   Does not bargain,
   Does not conspire ill will.

The Heart invites hard times,
   Has no defense against dark clouds,
   Wears no armor in pursuit
     of love or possibilities,
   Does not lie,
   Does not retreat,
   Does not hide behind closed doors.

The heart is a fighter,
   Knows not the meaning of defeat,
   Knows not the meaning of
     softening blows,
   Does not blink,
   Does not turn the other cheek,
   Is your best chance for happiness.

WHAT LOVE IS

I should write something.

A line that rings completely true; but then I'd wonder if there would be any left if I stole the last one for myself.

I should write something.

A rhyme that fits like the perfect cloud; but then I'd worry about where the next and the next and the next would come from and how it would fit into a world of imperfection.

I should write something.

A verb that moves like water cool and clear; but once you've tasted absolute simplicity, it's hard wondering what's to come, how it will justify pen and paper, and how I could deserve more.

I should write something.

A metaphor that needs no explanation; but that seems like the end, not the beginning, the sun setting on the longest day of the year, a valley sprinkled with glitter, glitter made of gemstones, gemstones too precious to see.

I should write something.

I would if I knew you'd read it.

YOURS ALONE

It's not my truth to tell.
Your heart speaks, but only to you.
The magic that sweeps you off your feet
   is magic no one will ever know;
   it is yours alone.
The castle that your soul manifests
   belongs to no man.
The treasure hidden in the corridors of your mind
   can be opened with a key only you can wield;
   wield it well.

It's not my secret to share.
Your tribe knows, but only they do.
The whisper that comes unexpectedly
   is a whisper that resonates with you alone;
   the essence of you.
The lyric that fits your song
   fits no other reframe.
The orchestra playing in the recesses of your mind
   know only the songs that you compose;
   compose them well.

GRATITUDE IS NOT A SHADOW

Gratitude is not a shadow peering over your shoulder,
   blessing you with lyrics of well-turned praise,
   or perfuming the air with godly ambrosia.

Gratitude calls for action in the world,
   clearing thorns and black fear for a passing stranger,
   planting yellow roses on hillsides lost of color.

Gratitude draws on bent backs and hard-rock spirits,
   opening roads on novel thought and gemstone horizons,
   taking root in peals of laughter and tinseled tears.

Gratitude lives in the memory like the scent of dawn,
   carves its existence out of revolution, evolution, and lasting love,
   stirring melody and song on heart-strings longing for home.

Gratitude leaves a man with more than he had,
   blesses a woman with love, light, and learning,
   touches a world with open doors and new perspective.

I AM LIEGE

I am liege to neither shadow nor storm.

I am liege to neither guru nor sage.

I am liege to neither boast nor brag.

I am liege rather to the trees of spring,
    to the perfect timbre of the nightingale,
    to the first blossom of the first rose,
    to the miracle of song and dance and the flame of life.

I am liege rather to the voices inside.
To the soldier who stays the watch,
    protector of heart, soul, and divinity,
    protector of brick, mortar, and the good bones of the soul.
To the woman who gives us balance,
    gives us fire, gives us beauty,
    and fuels a lust for new beginnings and a last and lasting stand.

Life swims in a river of choice and change,
    candles the torch of love and light,
    channels a gateway to a world within.
I am liege to all and none.

YOURS, MINE, OURS

Always the question…

Which of your many selves peeks out from the dark
   when all is dark?
Which of your many voices speaks
   when nothing but the truth will do?
What are the words you most hope to hear
   when motivation eludes you?

The wisdom you impart is wisdom
   only if it comes from the heart.
The inspiration of a selfless act
   will inspire for a lifetime.
The tenderness captured in a smile
   travels as far as a summer breeze.
The mastery you demonstrate is mastery
   only in the presence of humility.

Always the question…

   Whose wisdom? Whose inspiration?
   Whose tenderness? Whose mastery?

Yours, mine, ours.

DEFERENCE

Deference to the woman who
  stretches thought and emotion
  into a window of opportunity
  and honors for all to see the progress
  of spirit, kindness, and the cause of
  opening doors.

Deference to the man who
  fathoms the unfathomable,
  shoulders the burden of legacy,
  and sings the praises of youth
  and youthful thinking in a world
  bent on saying no.

Deference to the child who
  comes into the world free of labels,
  a troubadour calling for nothing more
  than long stretches of golden sand
  free of the tragedies and missteps
  of careless men and women.

Deference to a world demanding
  a fast track to peace and diversity,
  a thumb's up to cultures old and new,
  bridges as stout as free will,
  and what it means to stumble and fall
  and to get up again kicking and screaming.

Deference to you and me
  and to the long-held belief that
  much can be made of little
  and fancy is only a word
  for desires well-tempered
  and wisdom as open-ended as breathing.

PERFECTLY FLAWED

Picture someone close at heart.
Not infallible or without flaws,
   but a man or woman of moxie, free-thinking,
   and the ever-evolving qualities
   of an open mind, ingenuity, and going the extra mile,
   even in the wake of stormy days and harsh words,
   a fall we all know too well.
Picture them now,
   standing their ground,
   prominent like shadows at sunset,
   stride for stride with the stampede of hard knocks,
   standing tall, a meridian of fight
   and protector of the forthright.
Soldier, watchman, voice of reason.

Picture someone near and dear.
   Not unimpeachable or without fault,
   but a man or woman of savvy, enterprise,
   and energy enough to create worlds
   ruby rich in things sown of insight and innovation,
   even in the face of insecurity and poor choices,
   a road we've all been down.

Picture their faces,
　　deep in the knowledge
　　of life's many mysteries
　　and worldly enough to know that
　　goodness trumps anger and that action
　　fires the pistons of forward thinking.
Tiger, tender, lover of life.

This is not a perfect union.
Only perfectly flawed in its way forward.
All we can ask.

AT OUR BEST

Where is forgiveness in the pyramid of our truth?
   In the love we share?
   In our place in the world?
   In our view of ourselves?

Where is goodness in the actions we take?
   In the messages we preach?
   In the love songs we pen?
   In the desires that drive us?

Where is contemplation in the image we project?
   In the decisions we inspire?
   In the openness we reveal?
   In the changes that guide us?

Are we not at our best when forgiveness and goodness
   join in perfect sway with contemplation?
Is anything more pure than a moment alone
   with our thoughts, prayers, and passions?

HAIL THE CURIOUS

Hail the curious.
Hail the power of electric thought
   a million miles from settled.

Hail invention.
Hail the healing that ripples
   like jazz in a black hole.

Hail the teacher.
Hail the strumming of open minds
   and the channeling of new thought.

Hail the student.
Hail the challenge of dodging bias
   like arrows from an angry archer.

It matters not if the world knows you.
Only that you know yourself.

It matters not what the world has taught you.
Only that the path you choose is your own.

THE HEARTBEAT OF ACCEPTANCE

If you choose to travel a road unnamed,
    travel without baggage or strings attached,
    to the complications of connection,
    to the clothe of compassion,
    to the crossroads of courage.
There to find, explore, and illuminate,
    the art of affinity,
    the backbone of tribe,
    the silk of relationship.

If you choose to follow a drumbeat yet played,
    follow without time piece or reservations,
    to the percussion of intimacy,
    to the maze of commitment,
    to the elevation of virtue.
There to immerse, inquire, and scrutinize,
    the nobility of surrender,
    the gauntlet of team,
    the premeditation of mettle.

At the zenith of our exploration,
    in what often seems continuous siege warfare,
    we stumble upon the titanic of what is obvious
    and well hidden in plain sight:
    the heartbeat of acceptance.
Who we are, what we can be, the mountains we can move.
This is the road we travel.
This is the drumbeat that drives us.

A THOUSAND JOYFUL MOMENTS

This picture, like sparkles of fairy dust,
   dances through the open doors of freedom
   toward streams swift with promise.

This scenery, like waves of blurred vision,
   haloes the passage of princes and paupers alike,
   seeking, as we all do, equality of thought.

This silhouette, like portraits of long shadows,
   shapes all we know and hope to know
   in search of a thousand joyful moments.

We are the patrons of this promise,
   the royalty of new thought,
   the shepherds of this search.
All we can do is pay attention.

LOVE, TREASURE, DIVINITY

She spoke in verse so finely portrayed and delicately painted
   that only in a man's most honest moment
   could he unlock the wonder heard there,
   travel the untarnished pasture giving harbinger
   to opportunity as singular as a supernova.

We cherish those moments simply for their rarity,
   their galaxy of surprise,
   their invitation to travel among the stars,
   and the chance occasion to tie our allegiance
   to something akin to perfection.

If we allow it,
   there is no obstacle monumental enough to hold us back,
   no societal chant crushing the spirit,
   no guru poisoning the waters of clarity.

The prophet calls it love.
The pirate calls it treasure.
A man like me calls it a once in a lifetime brush with divinity.

NO ONE KNOWS BUT YOU

Every road we travel prepares us for this moment,
   this promise of today,
     these prospects for tomorrow.

Every lesson we learn signals this very course,
   this explosion of chance,
     this opportunistic thrill.

Every decision we make marks this exact turning point,
   this allegory of change,
     this metaphor for growth.

This is no time to look over your shoulder.
This is the heart of the river you're navigating.
Have been navigating since clocks began their ticking
   and seeds discovered the art of germination.

No one knows but you.
You are the sole report of things you.
The world is too preoccupied with courting favor
   and sifting manifestations.
They can't know you well enough.
Only you have that gift.

A BLADE

A blade cuts but it also mends.
A rock breaks but it also builds.
A hammer strikes but it also binds.
A gate traps but it also frees.

Without the arc of the diver
   there is no ballet.
Without the bending of the bow
   there is no arrow.

We stagger, but we push on.
We fall, but we rise again.
We run, but not before we walk.
We make haste, but not without planning.

Without vulnerability
   there is no connection.
Without the tapestry of souls
   there is no emotion.

A word wounds but it also heals.
A flame sears but is also ignites.
A wave crashes but it also inspires.
A fist closes but is also expands.

THE SIGNPOST AHEAD

I dive headlong, ever the fool,
   happy to be foolish,
   rash and blind with haste,
   treasuring these emotional explosions,
   these collisions with high hopes and keen anticipations,
   sheets soaked by a night cloaked in fantasy,
   fantasy colliding with the harsh
   reality of another day slaying dragons.

Reminisce not, says the signpost ahead.
Forget what's gone before.
Strap on your boots for a day bending nails.
Take a brush filled with color
   and turn your talents toward sepia-stained flowers.
Find a fast car or a broken-down bike
   and make war with the curse of standing still.

ALL LIFE BLINKING BEFORE US

All winds blow sonorous, resonant, electric.
Misguided, we bend our gaze and watch the ground
   rolling beneath our feet.
Lost are the nuances, the subtlety, the artistry.

Gemstones are called such because they come not easy.
Often disguised, always inscrutable, they are
   brushstrokes imperfectly rendered.
Found is the intricacy, the surprise, the relish.

Magnanimous the collage,
   a construct spellbinding and seductive,
   like ripples pumping discovery through our veins,
   feasting on moments we dare not miss.

Generous the portrait,
   a canvas universal and life changing,
   like magic as head-spinning as spice and intimacy,
   all life blinking before us.

I WOULD FOLLOW HER ANYWHERE

She, a prophet, a dreamer, a visionary,
   leading me with quick steps, a skip,
   a salsa, a laugh like fairy dust
     raining from the sky,
   the quick beat of my heart
     promising discovery, soul treasure,
     wishing well magic.

I love her imperfections and her dance
   and how much shorter even the longest
   road is when we're in lockstep.

I love the easy way she changes her mind
   and the way she sticks to her guns
   when nothing else matters.

I love the way she grips my hand,
   when lost,
   when searching,
   when hiding seems the only answer
   and the only thing she refuses to do.

I would follow her anywhere.
In ways only a fool would dare explain.
To places only a fool would refuse to go.
I would follow her anywhere.

NO PLACE

No place for equivocation.
No place for the mirage of being
  true to one and only one way
  of thinking.

No place for institutions.
No place for building walls
  when bridges lead to chance encounters,
  open roads, and new horizons.

No place for revisionist history.
No place for throwing stones
  and trading free discourse and hard truth
  for a deaf ear and a blind eye.

No place for the provocateur.
No place for rabble rousing
  when the cause of coming together
  is the hardest job we'll ever face.

No place for rumination.
No place for second guessing
  when what's done is done
  and the only way forward is forward.

EASY

I know I've seen dark around far too many corners.
Unkind how the mind plays its relentless tricks.
Unharnessed, another trap beneath another rock
   beneath another perfect lie.

Then there is choice, calling to you,
   like a cool breeze casting its spell in the heat of summer,
   like a smile on the face of exactly the right person,
   like a path that stares into the heart of true friendship.

Should be easy. But easy is not.
Is not a word that rolls off the tongue.
Is not waiting at the foot of the bed.
Is not a blank canvas inviting a palette of vibrant colors.

Easy only has its moment when you journey inside,
   harken to the message of jewels and harmony,
   trust to the river fast and reckless,
   embrace the prick of the thorn
     and the ambrosia of time waiting patiently.

HUMILITY

Humility is not the art of underwhelming,
Not a prayer in search of lyrics,
Not a portrait dashed in muted colors,
Not a shrug of the shoulders,
  an 'ah-shucks' tip of the head,
  or a broken-down Pontiac.

Humility is a realization,
  transparency, self-love, self-honesty,
  a mission statement bent on standing tall
    and standing back.
Humility is a jog on an open beach,
  a swim in a high mountain lake,
  a Sunday stroll through the countryside,
  doing the right thing when no one is looking,
  being the one person who fits you to a tee.

VERACITY

Veracity takes no prisoners.
Hiding from the reflection of what we see in the mirror
   gives rise to the most difficult battle we will ever wage.
Veracity frowns upon the waving of white flags
   and shuns the easy and oft traveled road to surrender.
Better to try and fail.

Veracity knows no limits.
Relentless it is in denying us the pleasure of creating
   false realities when it suits our purpose.
Veracity can be the best friend you'll ever have
   or an unforgiving enemy with no holds barred.
Better to stand your ground.

Veracity has no rivals.
Doing the right thing in the presence of none but you
   tests the depth of who we are and want to be.
Veracity leads us to the highest of highs
   and sprinkles humility in the garden of our growth.
Better to embrace it.

STREAM

There is a stream,
   like a perfectly imperfect staircase,
   tending to our every need,
   spreading seeds,
   and running dry only when the task is complete,
   forgotten, or unimaginably abandoned.

This stream runs through the veins of every child,
   and every child who stands for a changing world,
   stands before us,
   bearing witness to our deeds
   and paying tribute only when those deeds
   turn to the art of heavy lifting.

The stream is more than metaphor,
   more than hyperbole,
   more than deeds and heavy lifting.
It is that which propels us,
   compels us, completes us,
   gets us off the couch and out the door,
   and into the grind of a changing world.

RISING ABOVE

Herald the news of freedoms found
   and carried like a flashpoint to rooms locked
   by the stranglehold of fear
   and the mistaken notion that hiding
   somehow nurtures peace
   and foreshadows purpose.

Herald the passing of time-weary beliefs
   stepping on the throat of a playing field
   leveled by common sense
   and higher conscious thinking,
   sweeping the broken and willful
   into the beautiful black hole of bias and triviality.

Herald the reality of our limitations,
   the bane of weary folk wrestling
   hour, day, and year into decades and centuries
   with the urgency of growth and change,
   wrestling an opponent named human nature,
   and embracing the God given challenge of rising above.

TRINITY OF LOVE

It's not my choice to march from here to the holy
   place inside your heart.
It's not my choice to arch my back and hail
   the wonders of your song.
It's not my choice to cast away my mooring and
   trust the communion of two souls.

And yet I would spare neither tears, laughter, nor purity
   to know the searing and the sweetness of
     that foreign land.

Such is the trinity of love.
Such is the windfall of an open mind,
   and the good fortune of saying yes.
Such is the sacred ground of opportunity,
   the willingness to put one foot in front the other,
   and the glory of believing in yourself.

I will walk that road forever blessed.

THIS FOREVER

Shortsighted, when dawn breaks unheeded.
Tragic, when the eagle soars unnoticed.
Indefensible, when the seasons change unrecognized.
Lamentable, when wisdom dies unappreciated.

Did you miss it?
There! On the horizon.
A simple boat,
   wooden and worn,
   chipped and silent,
   a tossed and tattered sail,
   a flawless wake,
   in perfect silhouette…
And a message as clear as gemstones:
  This moment, this breath, this forever.

KINDNESS IS

In practicing kindness in yourself
 you nurture a sense of authenticity.

In practicing kindness in your home
 you cultivate a sense of continuity.

In practicing kindness in your community
 you foster a sense of transformation.

In practicing kindness in the world
 you reinforce a sense of evolution.

In practicing kindness in the moment
 you encourage a sense of honesty.

THE TOOL KIT OF OUR HISTORIES

What is it we most protest, deny, defend, argue against?
All manner of flaws, phobias, and failings.
A landslide of pain, hurt, and ailings.

What blemishes do we most readily turn a blind eye to,
   rage against with stunning silence,
   take with us into the steel cage of life?
Are those not the very things we need most explore?
The very things that chart a course for new beginnings?
Cartwheels on the sand?
Backflips and handstands?
Snow cones and bumper cars?
Comets, nebula, and shooting stars?

We all yearn to understand the "who" in the "who are we" question.
Why we think and feel what we do.
Why we claw and scratch for what's true.

We all yearn equally to be understood by friend, lover, partner.
Why they care and why they don't.
Why they love and why they won't.
We tangle daily with our mutual histories.

Mediate the rough road of life by our histories.
Set sail for new and frightening horizons with the toolkit of our histories.

We are built, rebuilt, and left without mooring or lifeline.
Who architects this great and inspiring castle is the question of a lifetime.

A STORM RELENTLESSLY BEAUTIFUL

The vibrancy of love has but one reward
   yet mile after mile of jagged road,
   hard rain,
   and the search for silver linings and lost treasure.
The chalice of intimacy holds but single gift
   yet hour upon hour of lingering words,
   trap doors,
   and a maze built of give and take and compromise.

One heart moored to another,
   the gift of gratitude,
   like jewels worthy of an artist's touch.
Souls forever linked,
   the tracks of flirtation
   splashed across moonlit snow
   from a storm relentlessly beautiful.

GRACE IS BUT A SHADOW

It is as if the bridge from shadow to grace called to us.
As if the steps we took were heavy with mud and star-crossed.
As if the journey seemed to crest one hill of hard fought wisdom
   only to tumble upon a next and a next,
     each no less tumultuous, no less challenged, no less humbling.

And yet we pressed on.

After all, it is the steps we take that give us measure,
   not the roads we stumble upon.
After all, it is the soles of a man's cracked and worn boots
   that give confirmation of his passing.

Grace is but a shadow of all we seek.
Grace enough to move worlds.
Grace like a river, more sumptuous
   than cool water, more resonant than song.

How I long to open freely to all yearnings,
   all callings, all meditations.
How I long for the quick infusion of daring and depth.
How I long for the bridge from shadow to grace.

LIGHT CRASHING FROM HEAVEN

Light crashing from heaven,
   aspirations wrapped in the fist of God.

This is not an apparition blinking false caution.
This is not the deep-seeded pain of knowing better.
This light holds the promise of castaways
   finding themselves at last,
   glimpsing the offerings of life unblemished,
   tasting the spindrift of momentary joy,
   tears just this side of laughter,
   and solace halfway to honest discovery.

Are there any among us strong enough to open their hearts
   and sacrifices their defenses?
Are there any in the here and now willing to walk the path
   of merit and high order?

Only the foolish and faint of heart
   would deliberately give up the chase
   without knowing themselves better,
   without exploring the deep well of self-worth,
   without bowing to the beauty
   of this light forever crashing from heaven,
   a friend, a teacher, a willing accomplice.

HOPE IS NOT WHAT HOPE IS

Hope is not global.
Hope is not a bent back spearing hard dirt with pick and ax.
Hope is not the search for the easy way out or the only way in.
Hope is not a finish line dipped in foreboding
   or carved in the black heart of space.

Hope is our personal universe.
Hope is a seed cast across a field of broken earth.
Hope is the memory of one smile from now until apocalypse.
Hope is racing for the pure joy of knowing
   that for every end there is a new beginning.

Hope is not an ace of spades.
Hope is not rain in the face of all out drought.
Hope is not a cherry blossom before a hard snow.
Hope is not a magic wand and the guarantee of a happy ending.

Hope is a color known only to you.
Hope is a masterpiece only your eyes can truly see.
Hope is the gift of facing every day with a plan.
Hope is you and me and a path charged with possibilities.

Hope is not what hope is but rather all we hope for.

WHAT MAKES ENDS MEET

What makes ends meet
   won't be answered in a heartbeat,
   nor a chain reaction,
   nor a pebble lost at sea.

What makes ends meet
   is the pressure building in your chest,
   the mountain rising up before you,
   the wisdom of knowing that
     nothing is known.

What makes ends meet
   won't be discerned in sleepy reverie,
   nor a sidelong glance,
   nor the last breath of fall.

What makes ends meet
   is the voice you hear in the dark of battle,
   the castle melting at your feet,
   the epiphany of learning that
     all is at your fingertips.

MISSING PIECES

Missing pieces.
Not missing at all.
Misplaced,
   intentionally so,
     in places blind and buried,
     places everyone sees but me.

I only see them when I'm breathing.
In the shock of being, whispered tongues.
In the winds of chaos, silent drums.

Chaos; it was once my freehold,
   once my soul mate,
   once my ship of fools.

Rain smells different now.
I don't hide between the drops.

———

(For David)

THE RUINED SIDE

I've seen the ruined side,
   traveled a path carved of misgivings,
   loitered in castles left for dead,
   scaled mountains long in decline.
Not lost, not searching,
   only choices poorly made.

I've seen the ruined side,
   catered to the scud monsters,
   lingered among rock fields,
   erected spires of discontent.
All of my own making,
   all stops along a road called necessity.

This alliance, long in the making,
   stirred a new way of thinking.
The hawk gave me wings.
The trees gave me moorings.
The sun gave me vision.

The ruined side runs deep,
   always a glance away,
   always calling,
   always tempting.

Changing the world begins with acceptance,
   of your many sides.
   of changing tides,
   of a clawed hammer and rusted nails.

There is always the ruined side,
   blinking cold reminders
   and leaving its calling card.
Embrace it or not, dance the dance or set sail.

Before I saw the raven.
Now I see the swan.

A CHANCE MEETING

Desire is that questionable friend who walks
    a fine line between yearning and hard truth,
    as all prideful lords and ladies do
    when crazy loose ends stare us down.

Pride dons the clothes of finely tailored accord,
    chasing the broken whispers of sailors
    lost at sea and herds of buffalo
    stampeding toward hard-fought glories.

Glory etches upon our spirit, for all to see,
    inexhaustible and incorruptible
    patterns of paper-thin disguises,
    a chance meeting of soul and self-honesty.

Yet beyond the bluster of these,
    this race toward desire, pride, and glory,
    refusing to be ignored,
    lives the questions that challenge
    even the most intractable of us.
What moves you in the long view?
What lodestone in the here and now calls to you?
What thing shapes you, prods you, drives you,
    and beckons a life worth living?

THEN

Run as far as your legs will take you,
   Then take another step.

Give as much as your means will allow,
   Then give of yourself.

Glean as much knowledge as will fill your head,
   Then realize that knowing is not knowing.

Love as deeply as your heart will allow,
   Then find the real source of your love.

BECKON CALL

Poignant then this message of survival.
Winter crashing like dominoes in shock
   and spring's none-too-soon arrival.
Summer churning like concertos and rock
   and autumn's long last beckon call.

Forced to see, we summon our downfall.
Learning to see, we invite a windfall.
Choosing to see, we welcome the historical.
Colors named, heavens tamed, sight restored.
Chains broken, doors opened, bridges forged.

Poignant then this flood of truth fleeting.
Lakes shimmering the unsolved and untapped
   and oceans symphonic meeting.
Rivers bursting with heavy metal and rap
   and streams dancing the dance of heeling.

Forced to be, we can't but stumble and fall.
Learning to be, we grow despite it all.
Choosing to be, we rise above it all.
Work and play, night and day, obstacles razed.
Boots on the ground, ever on, trails blazed.

FAITH IS THE MAP WE NEVER LOSE

I saw a bluebird the color of ocean spray.
   Sapphire, lapis, and cerulean.
I saw a monarch the color of sunrise.
   Sandstone, amber, and tangerine.

You may know this bird in flight, as I do.
He is a part of me, as he is a part of you.
You may have seen this sunrise and all it signifies.
It is the search we know as the search for divinity.

Does the world outside your door intimidate?
Cause you to pause, to question, to isolate?
We all spar with demons,
   but I wonder if the bluebird does?
We all run from broken clouds,
   but I wonder where the monarch goes.

I think of you with every pen stroke.
You live in every word
   and every space between the words.
It may be hard to love a journeyman,
   but the journey is where the magic lives.

Faith is not an option.
Faith is the map we never lose.

A ROAD OF A THOUSAND PITFALLS

That single day,
   when snow bled the earth
   of its color.

Hand over my heart, a pledge
   to carry myself from one stumble to the next,
   upright and convinced, even in moments when
   being convinced seems impossible.

Therein lies the linchpin of a solar system
   built upon fear's coiled and calculating claw.

He who vacillates holds no sway.
He who interferes builds resentment.
He who desires more than the hope
   of shedding his desires
   travels a road of a thousand pitfalls.

SOME THINGS COME SLOW

I am slow at this…
This feathering through
   clouds spun of chance
   and opportunity.
This willowing in pools
dappled in Shakespearian words
   and Rumi thoughts.
This caroling with voices
   joined by circus refrains
   and pearled rhymes.

Exploring shores in lands
   mystical and alluring.
Repairing broken roads
   and broken souls.
Chanting incantations of
   birth and long life.
All will have to wait…

I am finding myself so I can find you.
I am reveling in me so I can revel in you.
Some things come slow.

A THOUSAND TRANSFORMATIONS

Glistening notes of hardship
   tinsel the branded lines
   of a shop-worn face,
   suspicious eyes so out of place.

Who looks into these eyes
   without turning away
   less a decided sense of fear,
   impatience and retreat so clear?

Who looks into these eyes
   and offers redemption,
   directions home or a helping hand,
   breadcrumbs or a grain of sand?

Change is the one companion we cannot shake,
   the one record we cannot scratch,
   the one nail we cannot misuse,
   and change hinges as much upon
   purpose ignored as purpose pursued.

It is said that the fires of transformation
   are easily lit but difficult to stoke.
It is said that it takes a thousand transformations
   to herald an evolution as rough
   as uncut diamonds,
   yet but a single transformation
   to deliver each and all, man, woman, or child,
   back into the arms of blue-sky magic
   and the will to succeed.

THE DAY AFTER I SAW YOUR FACE

The day after I saw your face
   the road from here to there
   held promise unbound,
   stirrings uncharted,
   a place where no place once existed.

The day after I saw your face
   the wind blew cool
   and smelled of ginger,
   a blue like no other blue touched the sky,
   castles rose above the shore.

The day after I saw your face
   worlds both new and magical
   opened up to me,
   nothing seemed impossible,
   and everywhere I turned
   a door opened and light poured through.

The day after I saw your face
   a new freedom washed over me,
   and the simplest phrase evoked a melody
   sung from a mountain crowned
   in blossoms colored by rainbows.

The day after I saw your face
   I needed few words,
   and those I did went deep into my soul,
   and my soul sparkled
   like raindrops in the sun.

THE ALCHEMY OF DECEPTION

We are what moves within us.
We preach what moves within us.
We are possessed by what moves within us,
   and we remain forever its captive.

And then there is the alchemy of deception.
A missionary force guiding one hand in
   contradiction to the other,
     grappling with the synergy of fact and verity.

Where do we run?
Behind which doors do we hide?
Do we choose indecision or indifference
   or do we choose the elevation of spirit?
Do we give in to the alluring hand of fear
   or take a last stand in favor of deliverance?
Do we drink from the wishing well of delusion
   or fill our quiver with arrows of spunk and daring?
Do we make peace with the alchemy of deception
   or strap on the armor of resilience?

A HAVEN KNOWN AS FREE WILL

There is a place where skullduggery
   and the slippery slope of asking too much
   call home.

There is a place where villainous thought
   and the pure joy of wishful thinking
   live side by side.

Fantasy is alive and well inside the ticking
   clock of skullduggery and villainous thought.

Lip service is the perfect bedfellow
   to wishful thinking and asking too much.

We can choose to lose ourselves at this
   impeccably adorned crossroads,
   filled with dollar signs and bluster:
   easy enough.

But there is another choice,
   down the block and across the street
   from a haven known as free will:
   no need to knock.

ALL EYES

All eyes the crossroads.
All eyes the path to redemption.
All eyes the will to move forward.
All eyes the road the ahead.

All eyes shouldering the load.
All eyes treasuring the good fight.
All eyes spearheading a rebellion.
All eyes on the muse who inspires.

All eyes on the task at hand.
All eyes on questions never asked.
All eyes on the race toward connection.
All eyes on she who casts a wide net.

All eyes on the long haul.
All eyes on the moment of truth.
All eyes on the bellwether of change.
All eyes on genesis well-nigh.

All eyes on innuendo.
All eyes on the fast lane.
All eyes resolute and valiant.
All eyes on the steel toe of tyranny.

All eyes on euphemism.
All eyes blinking toil and tears.
All eyes holding to hard truth.
All eyes searching true north.

All eyes the aberration.
All eyes the good and holy path.
All eyes on staying afloat.
All eyes on the expedient:
   A world of equals.
   Fair skies.
   Food and water.
   All eyes.

I'LL LONG NO LONGER

She closed her eyes.
"I've dreamed my last dream."
Closed her eyes and swept away a last and final tear.
"I'll long no longer."

Trees grew outside my window.
We spoke of simple pleasures, things that made us laugh.
They wept when at last the shades were drawn,
   but morning brought a return to song and dance
   and horizons charged and filled with promise.

She crossed her arms.
"I've glimpsed the future."
Drew her shoulders proud and sighed a last and final sigh.
"I'll long no longer."

Children played outside my window.
We shared a trusting glance, one that lives forever.
They fled when thunder shook rain from the sky,
   but the sun's return signaled a new day
   and marvels steeped in skylark and frolic.

A DAY AS BEAUTIFUL AS YOU

A light as bright as any star
   flashes in your path.
Only the heavens could have
   tendered such a gift,
   rendered such lasting aftermath.

The moment speaks of its own rarity,
   manifests with time honored clarity.
It will not be held captive
   by the shackles of the past,
   nor the future in all its obscurity.

The moment is true.
Celebrations as bright as the day is new.
Treasures as rich as the sky is blue.
It is and always will be,
   a day as beautiful as you.

GOODNESS IS WHAT THE MAN ON THE CORNER IS SELLING

Goodness is what the man on the corner is selling.
   You can see it in his smile.
He holds court with butterflies and honey bees.
He hums a song written by goldsmiths and angels.

Gratitude is what the rooftop troubadour is preaching.
   You can hear it when she laughs.
She crafts her notes from straw and cool breezes.
She dances even when the music stops and no one listens.

   The search is not for answers.
   The search is for questions.
   Not the questions that break us apart:
     the questions that bind us.
   It is a search worthy of men and troubadours.

Allegory is what the maker of worlds is building.
   You can read it in his eyes.
His tools are parable and observation.
He blends earth and fire with the Zen of simplicity.

Metaphor is what the sage on the mountain is living.
   You can sense it all around her.
She colors her message with levity and changing tides.
She holds you with her eyes and wins you with her smile.

The search is not for knowledge.
The search is for learning.
Not learning that confirms what we think:
   learning that sparks learning.
It is a search worthy of sages and builders.

WHERE THE WORK LIES

What is the fruit of benevolence
  if all roads bend into darkness?
How can music herald utopia
  when the notes turn to coal and fire before your very eyes?

How is there mirth in moonbeams
  if thunder and lightning shadow the journey?
Who regales the winds of change
  when the crumbs of discovery ignore the burning bush?

That's where the work lies.
That's when you stand your ground.
Brick and mortar, chisel and saw,
  open the door and you're found.

SPEAKING LIKE SONG

How did it come to be,
  you and me,
  when hope,
  like water,
  so often spills from dams broken and lost of hope.

How did we chance,
  stop and glance,
  when faith,
  like shadows,
  so often melds into places dark and void of faith.

That alone is worthy of celebration,
  worthy of marble and bronze,
  worthy of running for home.

Home, where you are.
Peace, pearling the air.
Place, like a tabernacle.
Life, speaking like song.

FIVE, FOUR, THREE, TWO, ONE

Five is a calling card, a slow trek to the fast lane,
   the irreverent pursuit of balance,
   the echo of muted clapping,
   senses on high alert.

Four is divergent,
   less a force of nature than a safe haven,
   nuance and imagination,
   a scale for the common man.

Three is dialogue and divinity, shades of black and white,
   the trinity of chaos,
   the tinsel of tears coursing your check
   when nothing but tears will do.

Two is a tightrope, an arena of high drama and serendipity,
   hands clasp,
   twin flames,
   and the silhouette of two as one.

One is a call for companionship,
   a room filled with open doors and an invitation to breathe,
   horizons ravenous for chance and change
   with neither caveat nor quit.

VOICE REACHING HEAVEN

Voice reaching heaven,
   seeding anticipation,
   anticipation inspiring creation,
   creation filling a chalice of new direction.

At last, divinity on solid footing.
One story, one ending,
   and one truth at every doorstep.

Voice reaching heaven,
   tilling fallow fields,
   crushing doubt and reticence,
   dominoes of change spreading like brush fire.

At last, I've seen the eyes of God.
One people, one race,
   and the harmony of one chorus.

Voice reaching heaven,
   silk flowing into water,
   water crystallizing faith,
   faith at the heart of glee and possibility.

At last, the way home makes sense.
One direction, one road,
   and one world made whole.

BEYOND INTIMACY AND JADE

All I ask is an unlocked door,
   and a river-clear window into a world growing whole.
All I ask is a pitch perfect song,
   and an undiscovered path of milkweed and thyme.

Angels aren't necessary.
Nor revelation.
I'll take my chances with genuine laughter, a setting sun,
   and whatever the breeze has to offer.

I can travel universes without leaving your side,
   without opening new frontiers,
   just as long as the sunshine colors our window
   and the sheets are cool beneath a gently whirling fan.

All I ask are horizons near and far,
   and days heralding change and change gladly celebrated.
All I ask is an unblemished mirror,
   and a reflection true to every word we've ever shared.

Castles aren't necessary.
Nor starbursts.
I'll make my peace with cellos singing, cotton candy,
   and the tide peeling away the sand.

I can shape a river, stream, or lake with a hand on your back,
   a journey down the ripples of time,
     following the touchstone of here and now,
       and a brush with something far beyond intimacy and jade.

AN EVER-EVOLVING CANVAS

With you,
    the last mile is just as beautiful as the first,
    a work of art best described
    as an array of impeccably disjointed
    and imperfectly fitting puzzles pieces
    less concerned with staying inside the lines
    than blasting colors across an ever-evolving canvas
    where instinct and impulse
    out weight any need for order
    or any semblance of troublesome harmony.

THIS LONG SEARCHED FOR SIGN

Just so, this long searched for sign,
   wavering long and low and filled with apprehension,
   all flurries and drifting snow.

Just so, this long searched for sign,
   seeing canyons far too wide for mortal men,
   all calamity and rushing water.

Just so, this long searched for sign,
   looking back and courting a second chance,
   all rough roads and wildflowers.

Just so, this long searched for sign,
   bursting with aspirations and hints of light,
   all hard fought and worth the wait.

Every breeze holds secrets long on chance,
   ripe for listening, and fast becoming legend.
Every ship at sea has a destination,
   stars to guide it, and oars to steer it.

Ours to have and hold.
Ours to brand and liberate.
Ours to mold and shape.
Ours to make our own.

BUCKLE UP FOR THE RIDE

Today's truth is tomorrow's old news.

Tomorrow's old news spirals into a world of unpolished rubies
   or fast tracks a voyage to uncharted waters,
   time will tell.

Stardust never lies, nor does it fudge the truth,
   and the one constant is no constant at all,
   make no mistake.

The will of men can never compete with the forces
   of time and the machinery of inevitability,
   no use fighting it.

Turrets and battlements crumble and the hard facts
   of war and peace turn brittle in a torrent of backsliding memory,
   true enough.

He who pinches pennies is destine for a future of hard luck
   or a jamboree of silk suits, fine wine, and castle magic,
   no telling.

Right and wrong? Good or bad? Fact or fiction?
   These are no more set in stone than a swift moving storm
   on a sunny day,
   bucket up for the ride.

THE ONE THING

What is the one thing that stands the test of time.
Love like Christmas morning or a child's laughter.
A memory draped in all five senses and set in stone.
New birth, new life, a first smile and a last.
The music of her words in concert with yours.

What is the one thing fitting of a last stand.
The four walls of a place called home.
A hand held, a heart touched, a holy pursuit.
A bond like the letters of a newly formed word.
Equality like children see equality.

What is the one thing that stirs the deepest part of you.
A note rising from a chorus of passing birds.
A leaf falling from one tree to the waiting arms of rebirth.
An exchange of words sparked by passion and principles.
The master artist touching clouds and setting sun.

What is the one thing worthy of your last breath.
A rose pink and flawless in a stand of tall trees.
Allegiance to growth, passage, and perfect pitch.
All-in on this moment and what's to come.
A spoken word that need never be spoken.

TOO OFTEN

The oceans, the trees, the birds, and the butterflies,
   lodestones driving us to find our humble,
   universal place among equals.

We too often succumb,
   too often run,
   too often throw up our hands
   to forces intimating a willingness to accept
   less than we deserve,
   and far less than we should expect.

The right, the work, the honor, the strength of will,
   beacons pushing us to separate turmoil from
   the unstoppable energy of free will.

We too often equivocate,
   too often hesitate,
   too often play victim
   to our unbreakable selves,
   whispering "no" when we should be
   shouting "yes" at the top of our lungs.

INSIGHT TAILORED JUST SO

A wild aperture to the soul
   bursts open, stealing
   the black sheen of sorrow and rue,
   opting instead for a better version of right and wrong
   and triggering a fitting explosion of our world view.

Listening, as we so often do,
   to voices clamoring like discordant authorship,
   we hear a familiar chorus of naysayers,
   only to find a hand extended in friendship.

A shutter closed to the world
   breaks free, escaping
   the haunted halls of purgatory,
   and finding instead a terminal house of cards
   fortified with blooms of triumph and glory.

Longing, as we so often do,
   for runes of magic etched in iron and stone,
   we scale walls once thought unassailable,
   and discover a juggernaut of insight tailored just so.

THIS IS JOY

Like the sky, indelible.
Like the sun, inviolate.
Like the stars, universal.
This is joy.

Joy that bursts like a flame,
    not from a scene upon which you are thrust,
    or a play in which your part stands before you,
    but as a rush of song and limerick,

Joy that shouts from the rooftop,
    not from a note scribbled with predictable words,
    or a package delivered with no note at all,
    but as a portrait of zest and belly laughs.

Joy that spins like a cartwheel,
    not from a book written by an unknown author,
    or a song delivered with perfect pitch,
    but as a cannon of thunder and lightning.

Like a child, unblemished.
Like a friend, unwavering.
Like a mountain, undeterred.
This is joy.

NOTHING IS HELD CAPTIVE

This is not just a random echo in the forest,
   not just a foghorn raising a false alarm,
   not just a riptide churning in a restless sea.
This is the heart and soul
  of the beast
  guiding a dangerous mind,
  yours and mine,
  and the space left
  between diamonds
  and pearls
  and all we can fathom,
  provoke,
  and purpose.

Don't fret,
   there runs a deep river
   of red
   within your veins,
   keen, alive, and blazing,
   preaching, beseeching, instructing…

Nothing is held captive
  that is already
  bound.
How much fight is left in you?

MY LIFELINE, MY SPIRIT

This is my lifeline.
A lifeline spun of fibers strong in the way
   that only comes with the passage of time,
   letdowns, setbacks, and missed deadlines,
   triumphs, exploits, and unwritten headlines.
Like the sun to the moon,
   it is a welcome part of me.
Like the blue of the bluest sky
   and the hands of craft and artistry,
   it mends me.

This is my spirit.
A spirit sown of mettle hardy in a way
   that finds its footing in steel and grit,
   hard fought, mud covered, and made to fit,
   rebel, renegade, and occasional misfit.
Like the tree to the earth,
   it is a treasured part of me.
Like the wild of the wildest sea
   and the ships of lore and pageantry,
   it carries me.

THE ANCIENT WORLD

I've seen inside the ancient world,
   and all is not lost.
The ancient world where the only barriers to truth
   are the questions we fear to ask.
Where the only bridge to cross
   is the one between love and happiness.
Where the most beautiful flower
   is the sparkle in your smile.
Where the first transcendent moment
   is the last thought in your mind.
Where the mystery of discovery
   is the whisper you hear upon arising.
Where the only obstacle to relationship
   is the wall around your heart.
I've seen inside the ancient world,
   and all is not lost.

TO CAST OUR LOT, FEARLESSLY

Ever the vanguard.
Ever the one-eyed jack.
Ever a reckoning of facing facts.

A chant from the here and now calls to us.
A chance that never waivers falls to us.
To cast our lot, fearlessly.
To live with zest, effortlessly.

Ever the pathfinder.
Ever a call between heads and tails.
Ever the shock of blazing trails.

A chorus of give and take with much to gain.
A day of sunshine for every one of rain.
To reach for more, unflinchingly.
To ask for less, convincingly.

Ever the pioneer.
Ever our two-diamond luck.
Ever a time to be moonstruck.

A calling that comes as clear as arctic air.
A world view that speaks with truth and dare.
To stand your ground, defiantly.
To walk with pride, unapologetically.

HE WHO BREATHES CHANGE

They talk of quelling emotion.
They preach the perils of self-searching.
They call for the vanquishing of change.
They speak of knowing your place.

To flounder is no crime,
   nor taking a stand or speaking your mind.
To find yourself breathless only
   means you've chosen to seek.
To stir the well of candor and question
   only means you've chosen to speak.

A man who proclaims the virtues of not knowing
   breaks free of his shackles.
He breathes change.
He touts free exchange.
He embraces the stark
   and mysterious explanations
   of deep thought,
   quiet thought,
   empty thought.
He becomes a better version of himself.

BLINK THREE TEARS

Blink three tears,
    for desires that taunt you,
    for regrets that haunt you,
    for insights evading you,
    for prejudice jading you.

Blink three tears,
    in celebration,
    seeking, as you do, a beacon of liberation,
    a beacon endless and leading toward salvation,
    holding, as you do, to the task of healing,
    to fair play and the breaking of glass ceilings.

Blink three tears,
    for truths imploring you,
    for miracles awaiting you,
    for answers opening to you,
    for goals inciting you.

Blink three tears,
   for humanity,
   seeking, as you do, a river of opportunity,
   a river reckless and filled with serendipity,
   holding, as you do, to a palette of colors bright,
   to hard work, calloused hands, and the will to fight.

Blink three tears and be done.
Blink three tears and be on.

I YEARN FOR NORMAL

Words don't break the way thoughts do.
Words mean exactly what they say,
　　while thoughts twist like sugar cane in the wind.
I've given you my words,
　　but you're always in my thoughts.

Water doesn't impede the way rocks do.
Water gives life without protest
　　while rocks break the fabric of will and momentum.
I've tripped on many rocks,
　　but the search for water never ends.

A breeze blows sweeter than hard winds do.
A breeze lifts and soars and celebrates
　　while the wind fights and shoves and shackles.
The breeze pushes me forward
　　even as the wind pushes back.

Normal isn't black and white like turmoil is.
Normal mirrors the straitjacket of day-to-day life
　　while turmoil cracks open seeds of fight and fury.
I yearn for normal,
　　but turmoil is a closer friend.

THE SILK OF FORGIVENESS

Don't look long into the dark well of age
   and time passing;
   it comes without urging.
Don't wait for the day when giving a damn
   is no longer a burden;
   the good fight is all we have.

Loss, if we allow it, takes on a life of its own
   and loss plays no favorites.
Better to journey into a world where
   nothing lasts forever, but all has meaning.
Such a world seems an eternity away,
   yet rests enticingly at our fingertips.

I long for the comfort of a thousand fantasies,
   yet fantasy has an unforgiving half-life
   and its colors dim with time and exodus.
I yearn for the silk of forgiveness,
   a truer test of reality.
I hunger for the rough clothe of memories
   still clear and poignant,
   for the door leading to peril,
   and from peril to a world heedless
   of memories except the ones we make.

STORM THE GATES

How oft pilloried is the man of conviction.
How oft showered with stones.
How oft held hostage by misunderstanding,
   collar turned up against chilled gazes
   and indefensible riposte.

Follow your words.
Follow them with acts aimed at building, bridging,
   and sweeping aside fearmongering.

Follow your song.
Follow it with energy enough to topple mountains
   and expose the virtues you hold most dear.

Follow all that draws you near,
   so that following turns to leading and leading becomes
   the first arrow drawn from a quiver filled with doing.

Stand tall; a minute-by-minute proposition.
Walk proud; a one-step-at-a-time ambition.
Storm the gates of insecurity; a-not-so-easy conversation.

ALIVE WITH LYRICS

All of our best efforts are…
   dancing on the brink of chance and discovery.

All I know is in your eyes.
All I hear is a voice so illusively sure.
All there is if I care to see
   is a door swinging wide and inviting.

Life is the risk of turning away.
Falling is a chance to stand again.
Crawling carries with it the hope of walking.
Walking spills over with the rarified
   magic of taking one more step.

You give me the strength to breath that rarified air.
You paint a perfect picture of what the heart of the river can be.
With you, the water of life seems cooler and more tantalizing
   from one wave to the next.

I learn more about me in the reflection of us.
I journey into uncharted hues of soul and self
   and know the breeze is alive with lyrics
     only we could have penned.

DIAMONDS BRIGHT WITHIN YOU

Reap one act of goodness.
Realize one measure of kindness.
Demonstrate one act of valor,
    and thrill as the ripples of a new world merge
    with diamonds bright within you.

Once, there on the distant side of memory,
    balanced against one man's dream of fortune
    and future, came you.
You, chasing the quest.
You, traveling long into virtue.
You, setting free your inner masterpiece.

We all long to be more than our most
    frivolous dreams.
We all long to transcend what all others
    see as fantasy.
We all long for the wisdom of a child
    seeing the world for the first time.

Genuflect to the magnificence of the universe
>   and your place in it.
Spend this moment without expectations.
Journey without setting foot beyond the
>   sphere of your insight.
Be nothing less than the breeze tracing
>   the lines of cosmic thought.
Be forever more the diamonds bright within you.

NO NEED TO BE

No need to be a connoisseur of drama and fiction
   to understand the drama and fiction
   of sitting on the fence of life
   and lingering over the ramifications
   of sitting on the fence of life while the world slips past.

No need to be a medicine man selling lore and legend
   to disguise the lore and legend
   of swimming upstream
   in hopes of better knowing the odds
   against swimming upstream for anything better at all.

No need to be a sorcerer of spells and incantations
   to know that spells and incantations
   locked away in spin and sad songs
   can never free us from a history
   written from spin and sad songs disguised as good advice.

Truth is only half of the problem.
Truth pays no heed to bias.
It pays no heed to the color blind.
Truth is hard work, digging under the rocks
   of every tale ever told by connoisseur,
     medicine man, and sorcerer alike.

I SEE IT

I see it,
  perched on the feathered wing
  of a distant cloud,
  more veil than shroud,
  a picture perfect of beatitude,
    exaltation, and felicitation.

How wise can it be to canonize your thoughts,
  your fantasies, your castles built of sand
  and a playful hand?
How wise can it be not to?
Not to celebrate, rise above,
  and be completely you?

Hail the triumph over fear.
Hail the strength of vision, however unclear.
Hail heaven and earth and the communion
  of ten thousand living and breathing things.
Hail all you see in the only moment that is,
  a moment that shouts and dances and sings.

I see it now.
The starting line is all that matters.

FOR EVERY CHANGE

For every change,
   in the craziness that is our lives,
     amidst the cresting wave that drives us forward,
     there is loss.
For every mirror that we hold up to the world
   lives a reflection of the person
   we were before the juggling act of living
   brought us down to earth.

We know this much:
Change frightens.
It also enlightens.
Loss is inevitable.
Also indispensable.

Who we are in the face of change
   is not who we will be in the aftermath.

We also know this:
If every change provokes loss, it also ignites gain.
Something that was, is nevermore, neither good nor bad.
Something that is, continues to be, both full and rich.

If loss portends an upstream battle,
   gain suggests easy rowing.
Neither is true nor false,
   only pieces of the puzzle we call change.

PEACE AS CALM AS MEMORY

I walk the broken path of life
   to free a mind in overdrive,
   a mind that too often stalls and fails,
   too often races far afield
   and none too directed,
   colliding with misgivings and second thoughts,
   and manages, to my surprise,
   to land within shouting distance of a target
   I had only perceived in moments of pure fancy.

I walk the broken path of life
   to wake beyond the clatter
   and chatter and wrecking ball noise
   of a game called overthinking,
   trapped, as we all can be, in a chamber
   of locked doors and rusted windows,
   knowing that, just beyond my fingertips,
   lies the palpable hope of a breeze
   so enlivening and daringly cool,
   exploding with laughter
   and blessed with peace as calm as memory,
   as fluid as dolphins in full dance mode,
   as lasting as glaciers with memories not at all.

I walk the broken path of life
   intent on a world beyond the endless chatter
   and clatter of a mind in overdrive,
   only to find a path worthy of unlocked doors
   and opened windows and the palpable hope
   of laughter, peace, and memory.

NOW THERE IS TIME

Now there is time.
How much? How little? How priceless?
Are these the questions we should be asking,
  or is it better to know when enough is enough
  and to ready your sail for whatever
  the open seas have to hold?

Enough to recognize want from need.
Enough to cultivate flower and seed.
Enough to know satisfaction on sight.
Enough to separate dark from light.
Enough to swim in a sea of gratitude.
Enough to distinguish truth from platitude.
Enough to contemplate the question of why.
Enough to appreciate the blue of the sky.

Enough for relationships made of gold.
Enough for long walks and hands to hold.
Enough for unabashed optimism.
Enough for moments of altruism.
Enough for hummingbirds and tall trees.
Enough for quiet mornings and cool breeze.
Enough for the small things and the big.
Enough for the stream, the rock, the twig.

All for the good.
All in good faith.
All that calls us forward.
All we seek without seeking at all.
All we yearn for without yearning at all.
Now there is time.

DIAPHANOUS BLEEDS THE LANDSCAPE

Diaphanous bleeds the landscape,
   trapped in a tomb of closed minds,
   freedom moments from pulling up stakes
   and waving a white flag.

For me,
   it was not to be.
For me, it took no more than the gimlet eyes
   of forward thinking,
   the luminous smiles of children dancing,
   and a constellation view of love and life
   to raise a battle cry worthy of captains and kings.

Diaphanous bleeds the landscape,
   and neither deception, chicanery, nor subterfuge
   can mask the hard decisions of our past lives,
   give full meaning to the marathon of today,
   or silence the caterwaul of an uncharted future,
   mine, yours, and the worlds.

NOTHING CHANGES EXCEPT THE LIGHT

Beware of twisted words, like diamonds clad in stone,
   insurrection dressed as a helping hand,
   and throwing stones excused as tough love.

Beware of irreverence disguised as distinction,
   heavy boots masquerading as a midnight tango,
   and a dead-end laden with all the trappings of the silk road.

Beware the need to please charged with last year's insincerity,
   the urge to bargain less rather than bend a trifle more,
   and a wordsmith's charm hidden in sack cloth.

Beware of the status quo as a place to hide,
   boasting as a means of garnering favor,
   and the argument that nothing changes except the light.

DEEP WISHES

A smattering of deep wishes
    dwelling in a place nearly forgotten,
    left hanging like unasked questions,
    and buried like jewels in the folds of a drawer
    locked long before memory's sway.

All dreams travel a narrow road.
All roads defy whatever long-distance map
    the great explorers swore by, held to,
    died in pursuit of.
All maps forge a path true north,
    rarely challenged,
    long forgotten by those who see no more,
    yet a gift to those with eyes wide open.

What seeds have you planted?
How many hands have you held?
What living things have you nurtured,
    touched with your warmth,
      made whole their deep wishes?

LOVE HAS NO GUARDIAN BUT YOU

Love is more the act of knowing
   when to pivot rather than crash,
   adjust rather than calling it quits,
   ascend rather than falling flat.

Love rises from the celestial
   radiance of two luminaries
   instantly attracted, instantly
   on high alert, instantly in motion.

Love is a lifelong chain reaction,
   you holding your breath against the
   next tsunami of charged lightning
   and emotional free for all.

Love has no guardian but you,
   you in full battle armor,
   feet set in defense of life's
   most challenging masterpiece.

I TREAD WATER

I tread water,
   volition most prominent,
   ear to the ground,
   picturing the muse of color and light,
   that touch, that ferocity, that renowned.

Call it a crucible,
Call it a trial,
Call it the longest mile.
Call it a march through fires
   ignited by the unbroken will within,
   down a path traversed by the
   forebearers of everything we believe in.

You would be wrong not to take the throne.
You would be blind to the treasure.
You would miss the thread binding good intentions,
   there where the water runs pure,
   there where the ground grows fertile,
   there where the muse is forever tangible.

SOJOURN TO A NEW LIFE

When shadows stretch into the long
   and unsettled distance,
   it is truth that lifts us.
It is hope that sustains us.
It is spirit rising like a cloud, conveying
   us to places where goodness is a given.

We seek truth in places open only to our souls.
If a man is courageous in thought and deed,
   his soul reflects this truth.
Beyond truth is discovery shaking us
   into song.

Hope slips between our defenses.
There is no better gift.
The strong man opens his arms to this gift
   and fills his soul with colors few others see.
His spirit answers with divinity.

Our loss is his gain, sojourn to a new life.
———

(For Hank)

HONESTY IS

The lie came so easily.

It didn't have the power of fire, except
   to consume the fabric of my well-being.
It didn't have the mastery of water, except
   to change the ebb and flow of self-love.
It didn't have the luster of wood, except
   to paint the world in shades of gray.
It didn't have the complexity of metal, except
   to bend my will and distort my purpose.
It didn't have the strength of earth, except
   to shake my foundation
   and reward me with the gift of determination.

The lie came so easily and taught me so much.

Honesty is an orchid alive in the desert.
Honesty is a teardrop nurtured by the sun.
Honesty is the fruit of our revival.
Honesty is the wholeness we seek.
Honesty is.

FAITH CAN HOLD YOU

Faith can hold you,
   lift the shadows,
Ride the wind,
   cool the water,
Carry a broken heart
   to heights drawn
     in shades of mulberry and jade
     across the sky.

Hope can free you,
   fill the gloom,
Restore the broken,
   seed the valley,
Stir a dreary mind
   toward high adventure
     and the pursuit of onyx and coral
     shore to shore.

Faith births hope,
Hope spawns discovery,
Discovery sets a course
   to fertile grounds where
   love does more than survive.
It resurrects.
It elevates.
It flourishes.

GATHERING CLOUDS

Gathering clouds trundle
like broken stones across a murky sky,
and all I can do is give thanks
for their awkward beauty,
their petulant demeanor,
and the flood that will soon
wash clean a waiting world.

PLUNGE, MELD, SETTLE

Plunge,
Into the glorious arc of living,
With eyes wide open,
Into legacy and the making of maps,
Into the journey of discovering ourselves,
Seizing those chance moments
When a sense of peace
And calm
Allow us to see the godliness of life,
Those moments when the Body,
Mind,
And Spirit
Seem to meld together
In spark, fire, and harmony,
When the gift of serenity
Settles upon us.

SPLENDOR

Truth is not a matter of stealth
   or sleight of hand.
Not a train wreck or a flood of hard evidence
   in the hands of judge and jury.
Truth rides into your life on a wind
   powered by clear skies
   and voices in perfect pitch.
Waiting for a knock on the door
   or an engraved invitation
   is like waiting for the return
   of the good old days
   or a map in the hands of a lost traveler.
The splendor of choice and roman candles.

Truth is not a matter of evolution
   or changing times.
Not a thing you can box
   or a talisman in the hands of a gypsy.
Truth spins a mystical web
   illusive to any who give sway
   to fear and clenched fists.

Opening your heart and soul
   to the spectacular weave of
   insight and clear vision is all about
   launching a canoe into the swift
   and steady current of life.
The splendor of first and second chances.

LOOK

Look…

There on the horizon,
   beauty coalescing like a gift from God,
   beauty finding passage to your personal Camelot.

There in the eyes of a child,
   wonder melding with candor and song,
   wonder christening the open and knighting the strong.

There for all to see,
   goodness blooming like cattails in spring,
   goodness paving the high road for both pauper and king.

I know this.
Look, as you will,
  but know that life is no pasquinade,
  no triviality,
  no harshly penned satire.
Life glows, even in darkness.
Life rewards, even in sacrifice.
Life revels, even in defeat.

I don't cringe at the pangs of doubt and discord,
   the whispers of tough times and hardship,
   the rumors of spark and fire.
I seek shelter in your arms instead,
   there where nothing makes more sense than sharing
   the beauty, the wonder, and the goodness.

HOPE IS A MAGNET

Candlelight
   and the silhouette of half-empty wine glasses
     burst upon the ancient calm of memories best forgotten,
   best left to winters forever past.
Too often the wind breaks upon the perfectly formed melody
   of rueful song and changes the dawn into pitch-black
   remembrances of what we gave away.
Gave away without thinking.

Was it a question of insincerity or just a sharp learning curve?
Where were the wordless demands of fairness and trust?
Was it asking too much to offer amends and move on?

I drank from the cupped hand of optimism; I remember that.
It nourished me and gave the reflection staring back
   in the morning mirror the advantage of knowing that
   every gem ever created entered the universe with a few
   sharp edges and the need of some patience tending.

Peace, after all, is a puzzle long in the building.
Hope is a magnet gaining momentum with every step.
Love is an open wound forever on the mend.

I DON'T DANCE ANYMORE

I don't dance anymore.
Well, only when I'm not sitting down.
Or when the sound of music gets my feet moving.
Or when rain strums the rooftops like a snare drum.
Or when a bird breaks into song outside my window.
Or when the tug of imagination is too much to resist.
Or when good news is the highlight of the day.
Or when the sun comes up in the morning
   and sets in the west at night.

I don't laugh anymore.
Well, only when I hear you laughing.
Or when the trees reach out with their special magic.
Or when a child glees with play and timeless energy.
Or when the tide meets the beach and shouts with joy.
Or when friends gather with no agenda at all.
Or when fox and hound meet for tea in the afternoon.
Or when the stars come out at night
   and sparkle the sky like gemstones.

IMAGES OF PERFECTION

I tell myself:
   this rush of thought,
   this clutter of ifs and buts,
   this riot of imponderables,
Makes for a useless division,
   a tumble down one more broken road,
   a directionless side street,
   a dead man's curve,
An invitation to rollercoaster nights
   jazzed by sheets soaked
   in a crazy rush of fantasy and folly,
   mixed metaphors and carnival rides,
   and images of perfection
   too real not to believe.

MADE WHOLE AGAIN

Move on all you cousins.
Move on all holy men.
Move on all prophets of the night.
What is made whole again
   is not the province of preachers,
   seers, or kin.

Know who you serve.
Know what you value.
Know where the falcon hunts.
Know the monumental from the mundane.
Know the borders you have yet to cross.

Don't tell me you're angry.
Don't tell me you're trapped.
Tell me how the engines of heart, soul, and symmetry
   are made whole again by the most uncomplicated of motives,
   are made whole again by the tenuous ties of heaven and earth,
   are made whole again by shipbuilders and masons
   and carpenters simple and divine.

ITS NAME IS FREEDOM

Just saw the sign,
    wavering low and filled with misgivings,
    all diamonds and drifting snow,
    canyons far too wide for mortal men,
    a sign too pressing to ignore.

A sign proclaiming that every breeze
    holds secrets steeped in expectation,
    secrets fast becoming legend.
That all castles eventually crumble,
    burst into dust, rumble,
    freeing long-held aspirations,
    opening wide a world of interpretation,
    investigation,
    pushing man and beast,
    once trapped and unappreciated,
    toward enterprise, edge, and innovation.
A sign long trapped in a sea of harsh words,
    two-diamond-luck, and effigy.
Long overdue, this epiphany.

I can make this trek my own,
    breathing words too fine for mortal men,
    words far more apt for nomads and children.

Vision once blurred,
   purpose obscure,
   no longer.
And where upon fields come sprits and fairies,
   dancing the dance of revelation,
   reveals a sign long buried, now a beacon bright:
Its name is freedom.

SEARCH, OR PERISH

Where did you search?
In fields of snow as still as a painting.
In trills of song as pure as a summer's eve.
In bands of color as telling as a blushing face.

Why did you search there?
For answers as groundbreaking as new life.
For fulfillment as infinite as distant stars.
For ties that bind as permanent as forged steel.

What did your search yield?
Challenges as precarious as shifting sand.
Roads as perilous as the most perfect love affair.
Light as revealing as a straight line to heaven.

Search, or ask not.
Search, or know not.
Search, or perish.

THE BATTLEFIELD OF COMPLETENESS

Can I hold my head high, playing, as I have,
   with shadow dancing and the building of castles
   where none will likely survive?
Like a cautious but willing explorer,
   I walked into forests chorused in wind song
   and christened by the operatic sway of violins
   and heard the news of a world in overdrive.

We preach survival,
   but survival is not all it's advertised.
Survival is only fear poorly disguised.
Fear is only the ruling hand of the paralyzed.

Inside, the whole of me and its many facets
   steps daily onto the battlefield of completeness.
I am a warrior who so rarely glimpses an end
   to the fight that I have come to wonder
   if resolution is merely myth, mirrors,
   and mocking voices, somehow defenseless.

If so, could this war be won
   simply by staying the course,
   yielding never,
   and bearing the standard of completeness
   like a marathon runner with chest bursting?
If so, I go willingly.

THE PUREST WATER

Do as you will without expectations.
Accomplish that which needs doing without
   the thought of credit, praise, or approbation,
   and be grateful for your place in the background.

Do what you know is right
   when the only eyes upon you
   are the eyes of your many selves,
   and self-honesty will allow you
   a place where the purest water flows,
   and your last breath will be as towering
   and eclipsing as your first.

THE TRUSTED VISION OF HEART

Who are we who speak without
   the trusted vision of heart?
Who are we who speak only
   with the crutch of illusion
   or the blaze of futures past?

Nobility will, in time, move beyond
   the ilk of foolish men and fiction.
The foolish will, in time, hear the call
   warning against the toll of division.

Success is the elusive discovery
   that this moment is more essential
   than sweet song, than deep wisdom,
   than long words in search of principle.

Movement is a confident riposte,
   a sprint from tightrope to sandy beaches,
   dancing just to be dancing,
   a life of skinned knees and fresh peaches.

Triumph is a long bow and a sword
   and a target only you can chart,
   opposition only you can confront,
   and full faith in the trusted vision of heart.

NEVER A VENDETTA

Never a vendetta in matters of the heart.
Never the prospect of a head-on collision.
Never the thought of karma gone bad.

Only chance discovery of failings we all own,
   all who venture down the tricky
   and oft treacherous path where leaving
   makes less sense than staying,
   and staying is a proposition with trapdoors a plenty
   and poorly constructed passages in search of everything
   we've ever dreamed of and all we seek to know.

And for all that, worth every minute,
   every skinned knee,
   every stalled car,
   every crowded street corner,
   every show of gallantry and self-sacrifice.
Yes, even a willingness to stand side-by-side
   when the winds are howling,
   and the voices in your head
   are clamoring for a long stretch of golden sand
   and the soothing sound of the ocean at your feet.

Vendetta? Head-on collision? Karma gone bad?
No, just the hard and fast of a thing we call love.

TO SPEARHEAD A RESURRECTION

Maybe one hard and honest look into the face of reality
   is enough to spearhead a resurrection.

Reality invariably turns the corner on hard times,
   dangerous implications,
   and a rush of complications.
Yet it whispers in my ear and teases me,
   so easily,
   with a chessboard of daily exhilarations.

If I throw down all my defenses
   and race blindly toward its beckon call,
   surely I will succumb to unheeded traps
   and a well-deserved and inevitable fall.

Nonetheless, I urge my feet forward.
I crawl from beneath my favorite shackles.
Reality, not surprisingly,
   is painted in rainbow colors and stormy seas.
It has no boundaries,
   only a maze of circumstance and responsibility.

The maze rewards me with voices
   filled with substance.
The voices lay waste to my reluctance.
They signal a portal to a new direction
   and an invitation to spearhead a resurrection.

WE ARE ONE, YET TWO

She speaks with wisdom,
   a kind of insight laced in humor and challenge.
Her energy embraces both sun and moon,
   a universe stitched with silver linings.

She sees in technicolor,
   watching the world through a prism of brick and mortar.
Her majesty invites inclusion and demands respect,
    humble like a bird of prey in flight.

We met in a dream.
We grew in silent conversation.
Now we can never live apart.

I love the struggle.
I love the unity of our stride.
We are one, yet two,
  towers standing straight,
  leaning in,
  strong like steel,
  soft like water.

WHAT COST?

I could not have known. Not then.
Not without some insight into the flood of my own confusion.
Not without a glimpse into the panic spreading from limb to limb.

I ask myself:
What cost to the fallen angels who have shed
   so many tears picturing my return to the living?
What cost to the engineers of my well-being long
   dedicated to the revival of a wayward spirit?
What cost to companions left to wonder
   and holding out hope for a ship lost at sea?

We carry on our backs just enough fear to shake our confidence,
   but never enough to cast aside truth and consequence,
   as hazy as time may paint them.

What cost to reach out?
Could any act demonstrate more strength or courage?
It may be the bravest deed of my life.

WHAT HE THOUGHT SHE THOUGHT

What he thought she thought.
That of a world glowing,
   even in darkness and unsure times.
A world making beautiful rhymes,
    believing that he had the strength to fight,
    even the unwinnable, the unattainable.
That he was the answer, the medium,
   the drawbridge, the mender of all,
   even the unmendable, the unanswerable.
Hearing, he thought:
Act, be all, I need you.

What she thought he thought.
That of a river flowing,
   even in sadness and times of pain.
A river reflecting sunshine even in rain,
    believing that she had the will to nurture,
    ever the unavailable, the unassailable.
That she was the heartbeat, the middle ground,
   the way home, the lost and found,
   even the unreplaceable, the indispensable.
Hearing, she thought:
Be, be true, I want you.

The world, we find, is built on expression.
The river is nothing if not connection.
And the words we say or don't say matter,
   build and shatter,
   dampen and darken,
   enliven and sparkle.
Words well spoken, simply spoken, heart spoken.
Words rich, words strong, words open.

THE BIRD AND THE CHILD

Sits a bird outside the window box,
   its head filled with folklore, fancy words,
   headline news and gossip galore.
We were friends from the beginning,
   chasing scarecrows and phantom mates,
   and catching hell for staying out late.

Runs a child in fields alive with peonies,
   her thoughts driven by multicolored images
   and clouded with all sorts of mixed messages.
We were school mates and pen pals,
   playing four-square and singing outloud,
   and making fun of the in-crowd.

We label ourselves wise,
   always prized,
   yet long on intolerance.
We color ourselves poised,
   immune to the noise,
   yet crawling with fears.

We paint ourselves exclusive,
  even reclusive,
    yet longing for companionship.

The bird and the child,
  both teacher and friend.
Once the heart of our world,
  now a means to an end.

A FIGHTING CHANCE

The soul is where candor resides,
  there, in words spoken from a dais polished
  with the rough cloth of deeds and action.
And what we hear is a message too profound,
  that what we believe to be can so easily be turned,
  can so swiftly fall and fracture.

We use our minds to protect us from vulnerability,
  but the mind too often takes the easy path.
When it does, candor and love are likely casualties,
  and all we're left with is the aftermath.

The heart is where love shelters,
  there, in feats staged on a tether strung
  between pure foolishness and acts of bravery.
And what we see is a scene too familiar,
  that what we wish for is so remarkably elusive,
  so often the thing of knavery.

We use our angels to see the tie between heart and soul,
  and our angels rarely settle for the backdoor.
Because they don't, we're left with a fighting chance,
  and sometimes a fighting chance is all we can ask for.

BRAVING THE PATHLESS

Like the sorcerers of worlds archaic and misguided,
   we create fictions,
     myths, like the nets of the seaworthy,
     snaring the hearts and minds of lost and longing souls
     desperate for a thing or two or ten to hold as true.

Like the wool gatherers of the ten thousand tribes,
   we sow fables,
     rumors, like spinning yarn into garments of shadow,
     wandering, lockstep and lost, in bands of like-minds
     becoming more like-minded with each new tale.

Without myth, we are one, answering to the wind alone.
Without fiction, we travel free, bound only by the path before us.
Without hoards forming hoards, we crash of our own accord,
   soar upon our singular wings,
     choosing the falling rock to the avalanche of group thinking,
     choosing the oar of a seafaring skiff to the crowds of the carnival.

We write fictions for the masses.
We pray to the gods of a thousand manufactured myths.

We dismantle the fiction by standing our ground,
   even if it means standing alone.
We disprove the myth by listening to the beating of one heart,
   the heart of one man, one woman, one child,
   and braving the pathless.

NOW WE'RE ONTO SOMETHING

The dance with money signifies not a crowning achievement.
The illusion of power portrays not the capstone of a life well lived.
Luxury is little more than a word for wanting more.
Control is a poor excuse for not letting go.

Plant a tree.
Search out a waterfall.
Smile at a stranger.
Share a verse of personal reflection.
Now we're verging on an achievement worthy of celebration.

Build a bridge with your words.
Lend a helping hand with your actions.
Stay a minute longer.
Embrace just to embrace.
Now we're scaling the high points of something profound.

Listen like your life depends on it.
Dance just to feel your feet move.
Skip a stone.
Worry not about saving face.
Now we're turning the colors of life into a portrait of high art.

Author and artist Mark Graham lives in Denver, CO with his wife. For more, please visit MarkGraham-Art.com.

www.ingramcontent.com/pod-product-compliance
Lightning Source LLC
Chambersburg PA
CBHW061442040426
42450CB00007B/1168